Guess What?

Guess What?

ISBN: 978-1-910181-17-1

Published October 2015
First printed October 2015
Second Issue printed November 2015

Printed and Published by Anchorprint Group Limited

Enquiries:
The Urban Equestrian Academy Ltd
1 The Crescent, King Street, Leicester, LE1 6RX

Email: tfzampa@gmail.com

Website: www.hood2horses.co.uk

CONTENTS

ACKNOWLEDGEMENTS

I would like to first thank the 'Most High'.

Thank you to my Dad because he helped me out with my book; I would like to thank my Mum because she is the greatest Mummy ever; I would like to thank my brother's 'Che and O'Shae' because they gave me some ideas for my story 'My Brother's'; I would like to thank my sisters Atlanta and Morgane - Renee nickname Mogwie, for being my sisters, Aunty Es-she for the drawings and I would like to thank my other family on both Mum and Dads sides all over the world.

Lastly 'Big Up' my cat Pharoah :)

saw some animals like rabbits, horses pigs, goats and lammas. Later on we had are freezing lunch it was so cold that I got a brain freeze and teeth freeze if you have ever heard of that before. After a while it started snowing so it got even colder and there was a snow storm. Some kids were crying because it was so cold and huddled round this fire lamp ting.

At last we left and we had a nice warm journey back on the coach. Everybody was happy to leave because it was freezing. When we got back school everyone was handing out ice cream and all of our class got the ice cream for free and "GUESS WHAT?" .... yes us kids still liked are ice cream even though we froze all day!!

OUR HORROR HOLIDAY

OUR HORROR HOLIDAY

How did it start.............

Well it was the summer of 2012. Mogane and Dad had collected enough tokens for us to go on holiday, while Uncle Judah was collecting them too so his family could come with us. So we all booked a holiday; about a month later we all got dressed and got into our cars, we went together with Uncle Judah following behind us. Our cousin's Rimmon and Moorice and their mum came with us too.

It was supposed to take us 3 hours but "GUESS WHAT?", we went the wrong way so we had to figure out the right way! As soon as we did we got back on track
but "GUESS WHAT?" .... it ended up taking us 11 hours so basically the whole day!

When we arrived we had to sleep in our cars, my dad was scaring us by saying a Jakalantan was going to come and get us; a Jakalantan is basically a man with no head riding a donkey holding a lantern in his hand so obviously we were petrified, squeamish and squished in our jeep, while Uncle Judah and our cousins were even more squished in there little car. The next day we all went to the beach, my mum, Atlanta, Morgane, me and Shanell all stayed on the seashore while O'shae, Che', Uncle Judah, Rimmon, Moorice and my dad all went in this cave . A while after that the flood started to come in. So we all started to call their names and say the flood has started to come in.

8

Dad and Uncle Judah didn't believe us, they seemed to be ignoring what we were saying even though we was waving our arms crazily trying to alert them to the danger that was creeping up on them.

Eventually we could see that they we heading back out of the cave. It must have dawned on them because I could see Dad had O'shae in his arms and was now running out of the Cave with Uncle Judah as the tide was rising, at this point we was running towards them to help. Atlanta and Morgane held Rimmon and Moorice; I was running with Shannel, and Mum was holding Che, we were all at this point knee deep in water! We managed to escape just in time!!

After this episode we headed back to our cars visibly terrified from the ordeal our Dads had just put us through. Uncle Judah reached into his pockets and "GUESS WHAT?" ...... his keys were gone!!

My dad and Uncle Judah went back to the beach to look for the keys. It was serious as if Uncle Judah doesn't find his keys, he, our cousins and their mum would have to 'WALK BACK TO LEICESTER!!!'.

I was thinking Uncle Judah must have lost his keys in that cave when he was running out in a panic and if that was the case then there would be no way he would

OUR HORROR HOLIDAY

find them.

Whilst Uncle Judah and Dad were out looking for the keys, Rimmon and Moorice had to sit on our laps. Shanell was obviously not impressed and looked really angry.

Dad came up with an idea to take us back to the Caravan Park as we were now not only still shaken from our cave and tide experience, but also hungry and frustrated with the loss of keys situation. So we all squeezed up into the 7 seater and made the short journey back to the Caravan site. Dad left us here and went back to help Uncle Judah find the keys.

After a fairly short while I was happy to see through our window that Dad was coming back to the site in the white jeep followed by Uncle Judah in his black Fiesta. He had found the keys!

"And you know what?" ....
Happy Days ☺ he found the keys in the sand.

SOMEONE STOLE MA BIKE

SOMEONE STOLE MA BIKE

Why did they steel my bike.....................

Well it was a sunny day and my birthday was on February
the 17th so I think that is near the summer.

Anyways I wanted to ride my NEW!!!!!!!, you hear what I
am saying NEW BIKE!!!!!!! to school, so my dad and my
mum let me. So I rode it to school; after that after all of our
lessons I looked in the shed and my bike was not there!!!!!!!!
So my sister Morgane asked me if I took it to school because
she doesn't know because she leaves before us. So I said
yes I did. She said let's look at home because you might
of left it there so I said ok but I was thinking, I did take it to
school.

When we arrived home we looked in the kitchen and it
wasn't there so we asked our Aunty Jackie if she moved my
bike and she said no. So I ran upstairs and started crying
because I really liked my purple and black bike I got from
my pap's. When my Mum and Dad came back we told them
the news they were shocked. So my dad went to my school
with a big frown because do you know when you scrunch
your eyes when you get angry that's how you frown. So he
went to the school cool and started arguing with them. After
the argument my Dad called the police and they were on the
loose.

When the case was found the police asked her some questions. He asked her some questions the questions were these.......

Policeman: Why did you steel the bike?

The suspect: Because I wanted to and my daughter wanted it to.

Policeman: Does your daughter have a bike?

Suspect: Yes

Policeman: So why did you steel it?

Suspect: Because why not

Policeman: Do not get rude do you want to go jail?

Suspect: Shush I am trying to run away with the bike.

Policeman: What did you say?

Suspect: I am not repeating myself.

Policeman: Ok that's enough come on your going to the station!!!!

SOMEONE STOLE MA BIKE

Suspect: Aaaaaaaah

So after all the madness they took her and her daughter to court, they talked to her for a little bit and said we are going to search your house but she said that she sold the bike. They said you get the bike back or you will face serious trouble because we seen u take it on the school camera. In the end she could not find the bike so she got punished but I don't know how.

And "GUESS WHAT?" I didn't get my bike back and we did not get the money back ....But anyway I got another bike from my paps a bigger and better one pink, white and black, this time .

GREAT GRANDMAS HOUSE

GREAT GRANDMAS HOUSE

Every weekend me and my brothers go to are pap's
house but I do not want to tell you why. Anyway we all
went to our great grandma's house. When we arrived;
just to say we are Muslims; anyway when we arrived,
we kissed great grandma but I wiped it off, and we
went upstairs. We put our things away and we went to
granddads house where I never want to go anyway do
you know the story 'Someone Stole Ma Bike' it is kind
of connected to this because at the time i did not have a
bike and I was going to take my cousins bike from there
but the tyre had a hole in it. So we went back to Great
Grandmas when it was night time and we are Muslims
but she is Christian, we had to do the Jesus prayer it
goes like this.

Our fader,

bought in heaven,

di kin dome come,

di will be done,

on eart as it is in heaven,

give us this day and our daily bread,

and forgive us are tress passes,

Amen.

OMG Lard Gad. After the Jesus prayer we all go bed and have a nice sleep. The next morning me and my dad were sleeping and all we hear is............

Grandma: "Terrell, Terrell can me a come in"

Dad: "Yes Gran Yes Gran".

She don't say ma paps name right his name is Tariq or Freedom, its so annoying but most of all she stayed in there for like half an hour just to get a black T- shirt for church and "GUESS WHAT?" .... she always asks for half a cup of tea with some cold or hot water, I mean how can you have half a cup of tea and water, it's so weird.

CANDICHOCALIOUS

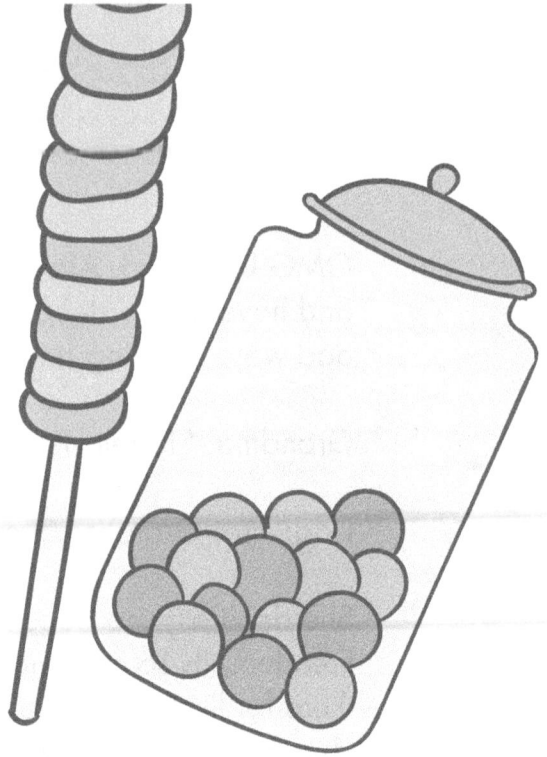

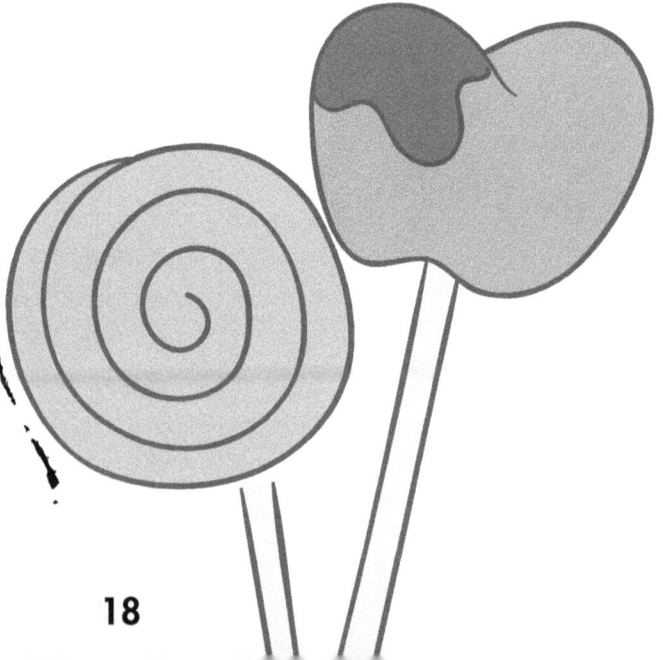

CANDICHOCALIOUS

FR33DOM

18

Me and the boys stayed at my Dad's for Christmas holidays. We are Muslim but we still had Christmas dinner. For Christmas dinner we had lamb, potatoes, rice and vegetables ummm so nice. After Christmas the boys went to Granddads but I stayed with my Dad, cus I didn't want to go Granddads.

It was night time after Christmas on New Year's Eve, I had been telling my pap's to stop smoking because he always smokes and it stinks. So one day we had a conversation about smoking so he said I have one left so let me just do my thing outside and I promise I won't smoke no more baby. So he had his last one and said bye to the smoke that floated away but I just slammed the door!

After we saw fireworks on television, heard some, seen some but we did not do any. And are Great Grandma went away to London with Aunty Hazel. So I kept checking if they were gone. When they were gone me and my dad put on Kabaka Pyramid Reggae Music and turned it up maximum power. We had the whole house to ourselves so we went crrrraaazzzyy!!!

CANDICHOCALIOUS

It was snowing during the winter holidays; we went to this shop called Candichocalious when it was snowing.

On the way there I kept throwing snow balls at my dad so when we got to the shop and brought sweets on the way back my pap's got a big snow ball and threw it right in my face. It was so cold I started to cry. When we got back we put are sweets into a bowl of ice cream and ate some but at the end we got full!

And "GUESS WHAT?" .....my Great Grandma did not come back for a week, and since then my pap's is still not smoking because I always check.

JAMEELAH NEARLY DROWNED

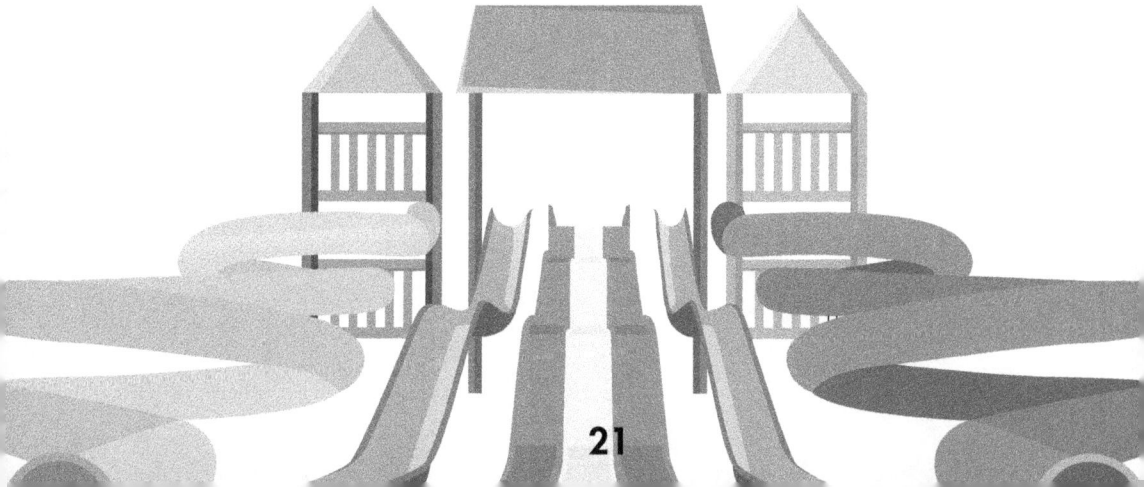

JAMEELAH NEARLY DROWNED

It was a sunny day because it was the summer holiday.
I must have been about 6 or 7, Jameelah was 10 or
11, Morgane was about 13 or 14 and my Dad about
34 or 35. Dad planned to take us swimming so we
could go down the water slide and ride the waves,
Beaumont Leys swimming. My sister Morgane, my
cousin Jameelah and my Dad all taught me how to
swim under water but I didn't get the hang of it.

So they taught me how to swim on my back but I didn't
get the hang of it as well. We went into the little pool
because we were in the big pool before; we went in
a kind of waterfall that was really fun. We went under
this thing that tips on you and you get really wet, so wet
that the water goes into your swimming boxers or your
swimming suit.

So after that because I couldn't swim properly they got
me some arm bands and it was much better after that.
My Dad went under the water and crept up on Jameelah;
he yanked her leg and "GUESS WHAT?" ....
She nearly drowned!!!!!!!!! Cuz Jameelah was now
drowning under water; he had to pull her back up as
fast as he could.

JAMEELAH NEARLY DROWNED

At this point Jameelah was in a bit of a panic;
with water streaming down her face he asked her
"Are you ok Jameelah, are you actually crying?"
She couldn't breathe properly and said "No am not,
it's just water all over my face". We did not believe her
because sometimes she lies or shall I say always lies,
but "GUESS WHAT?" after getting better she started
laughing so my Dad kept doing it.

"And you know what?" ....
I love my crazy cousin Jam Jam.

THE BOYS

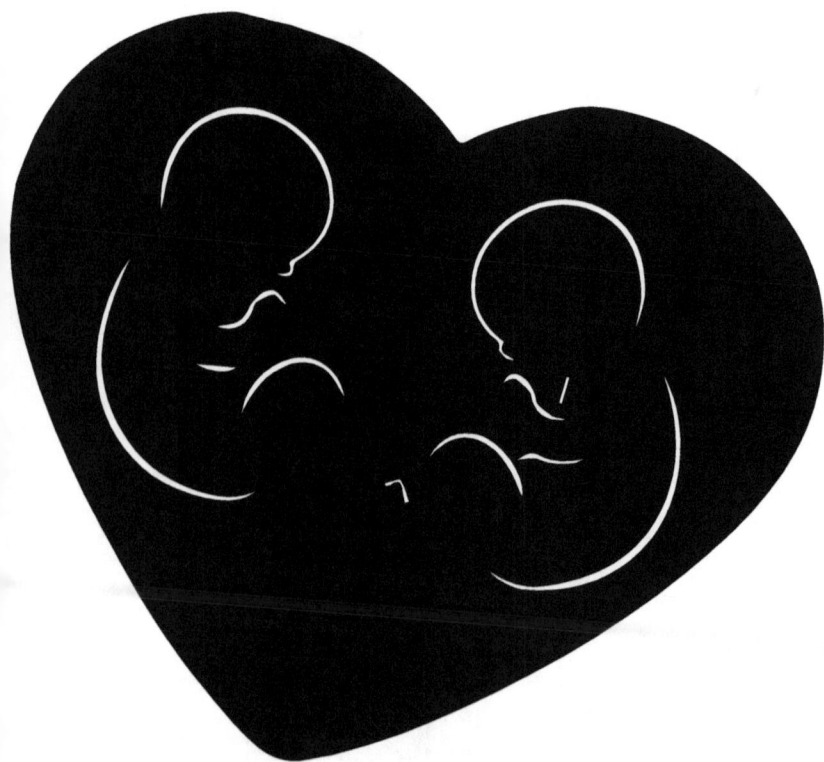

I have 2 brothers called Che and O'shae; they are basically twins; because they are twins we call them the boys. Che is 2 minutes older than Oshae. Che had to come out first because Osahe was eating all the food and Che was going Anorexic. Oshae is still a greedy eater. There nicknames are Oshaypoosh and Shadypop or Shadyman.

When Che was about 9 months old he had a hernia, which is when your belly button goes big and he had to go hospital for an operation.

They are both five, they both have glasses, Che has Brown Gruffalo glasses and Oshae has Blue Star Wars glasses and they both have the same clothes and shoes and they both look the same. When they wear the same cloths you can't tell which one is which and sometimes in pictures they can't tell which one is them. Only me, Mum, Dad, and my sisters know which one is which. Our neighbours Tia, Amara, Ash, Isa, Zara and Vicky don't know which one is which.

Che is more bad than Oshae but sometimes it's the other way round. Oshae is always doing naughty things though. They both like to play on the playstation they like Fifa Football, F1 and Boxing they like sports and fighting games, they are also good at real football, but they don't like to go school even though they say they do.

THE BOYS

They always help me but sometimes they don't listen
to me. Whenever they talk they like to say the same
thing and copy each other. They like playing together,
doing things together and helping each other. They
both like bugs and creepy crawlies but Che doesn't like
Butterflies.

On the weekend they get up at six oclock in the morning,
come into are room and say 'Morgane Morgane
Atlanta Atlanta can we have our breakfast now' which
is really annoying so mum always comes and tells them
off. These are my only 2 brothers and even though they
can be annoying "GUESS WHAT?" ....

They are still my best friends and I look after them.

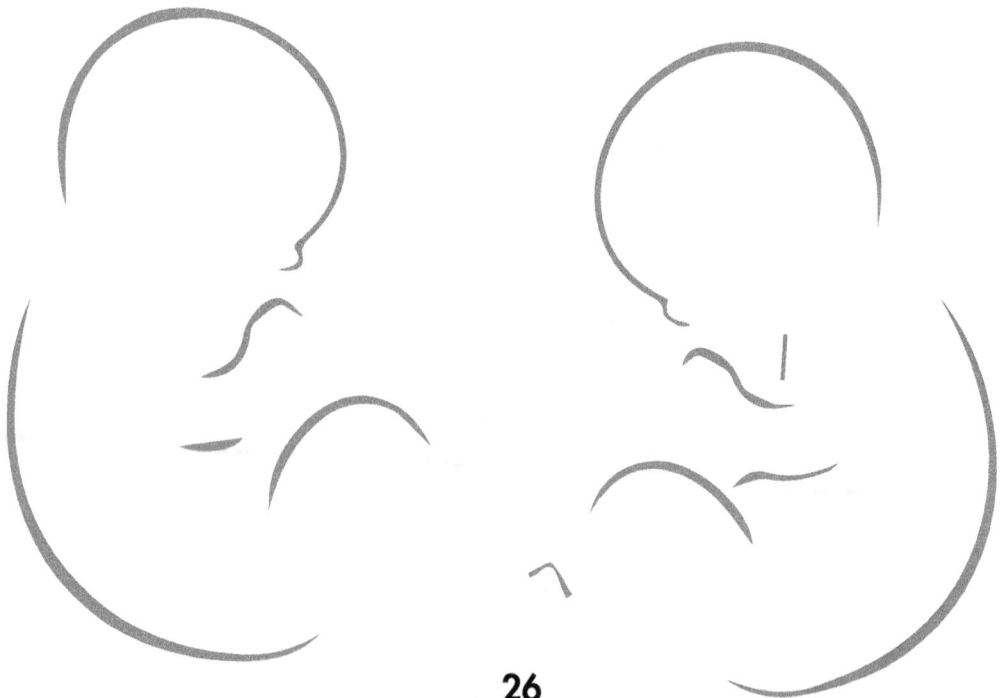

BIRMINGHAM WITH AUNTY ES-SHE

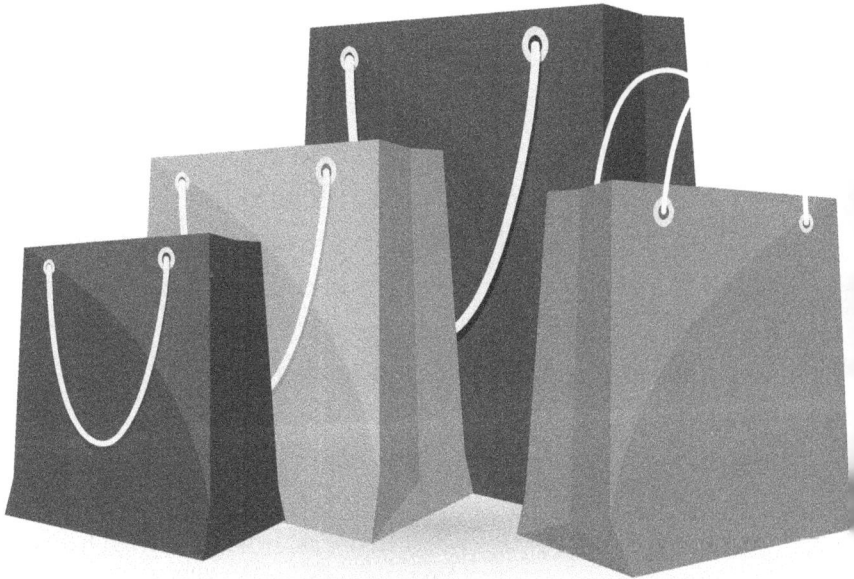

BIRMINGHAM WITH AUNTY ES-SHE

About 3 years ago when I was 5 my Aunty Es-she took me on a train for the first time. We went Birmingham. The train went super super fast; we went under a dark dark cave and had some food and drink. Our food was cheese sandwich and Ribena drink. It was so much fun. When we arrive we saw Mario and Luigi in suits blowing up love heart shaped balloons. After we saw the Mario and Luigi we saw this predator monster dancing and I was scared but I took a picture with it, but its armpits stunk OMG!

We went to a shop I forgot what it is called my cousin Jameelah bought some trainers, my Aunty Es-she bought some clothes and she bought me a bear purse and I have still got it. After we went to this donut factory and we saw how they make donuts and we brought some with different toppings on they were so nice. We went into this big tower and bought lots of sweets I can only remember these ones, purple skittles and strawberry laces.

After we went into a teddy bear monkey shop there were 2 teddy bears dancing listening to music Riana shut up and drive. I was going to buy one but my aunty did not let me. After we went into a hex bug shop toy bugs where climbing that we went to have our lunch we had takeout from a shop we had a smoothy with our food it was so nice. After we went to a necklace shop and we brought necklaces. We also brought one each.

After we went back to the train station and "GUESS WHAT?" ....we had a long jouney back.

FARM TRIP

FARM TRIP

It was early in the morning on a school day when I
never want to wake up so I was sleeping as always at
6.00 am in the morning and all I hear is "Azeezah it's
time to wake up or I will tell mum". So annoying; so I
woke up before my sister Morgane even reached my
mums room; tiredly I went in the bathroom with my dad,
brushed my teeth, had a wash and got ready. I had to
hurry up because I had a trip to the farm.

When I got school I went into my class room and most
of my friends where there waiting to go on the trip, we
was all excited. There was one boy in class whose mum
did not want him to go so he got super angry ran out of
the school but the teachers jumped on him and dashed
him in year1.

After the problem was sorted the coach came and
picked us all up and we were on our way. I and my
friends where hungry so we kept saying can we eat
now we are there. We went on a motorway. When we
arrived we did not see Shonah's mum at the back of the
coach. We had a talk then catched up with the class. It
was really cold when we got to the playing area and
we all went under the barn and swung on a rope.

Daddy lifted me on his shoulders so my feet didn't have
to touch the cold ground like the other kids. He walked
all around the farm with me on his shoulders. After we